To Tonya & Blake - thank you both from the bottom of my heart.
May your kindness be rewarded to you many times over for the rest of your life.

Catherine and Amy, I pray the world will know and appreciate your incredible talents as I have. I am so thankful to have found you both.

Sandiya, continue to fly fearlessly for everything you want in life. I love you.

Sightseeing with Sandy
Fun in the Bahamian Sun!

CO-CREATED BY
SANDIYA BADMUS AND SHAMBREKIA WISE

ILUSTRATED BY
CATHERINE PARAISO

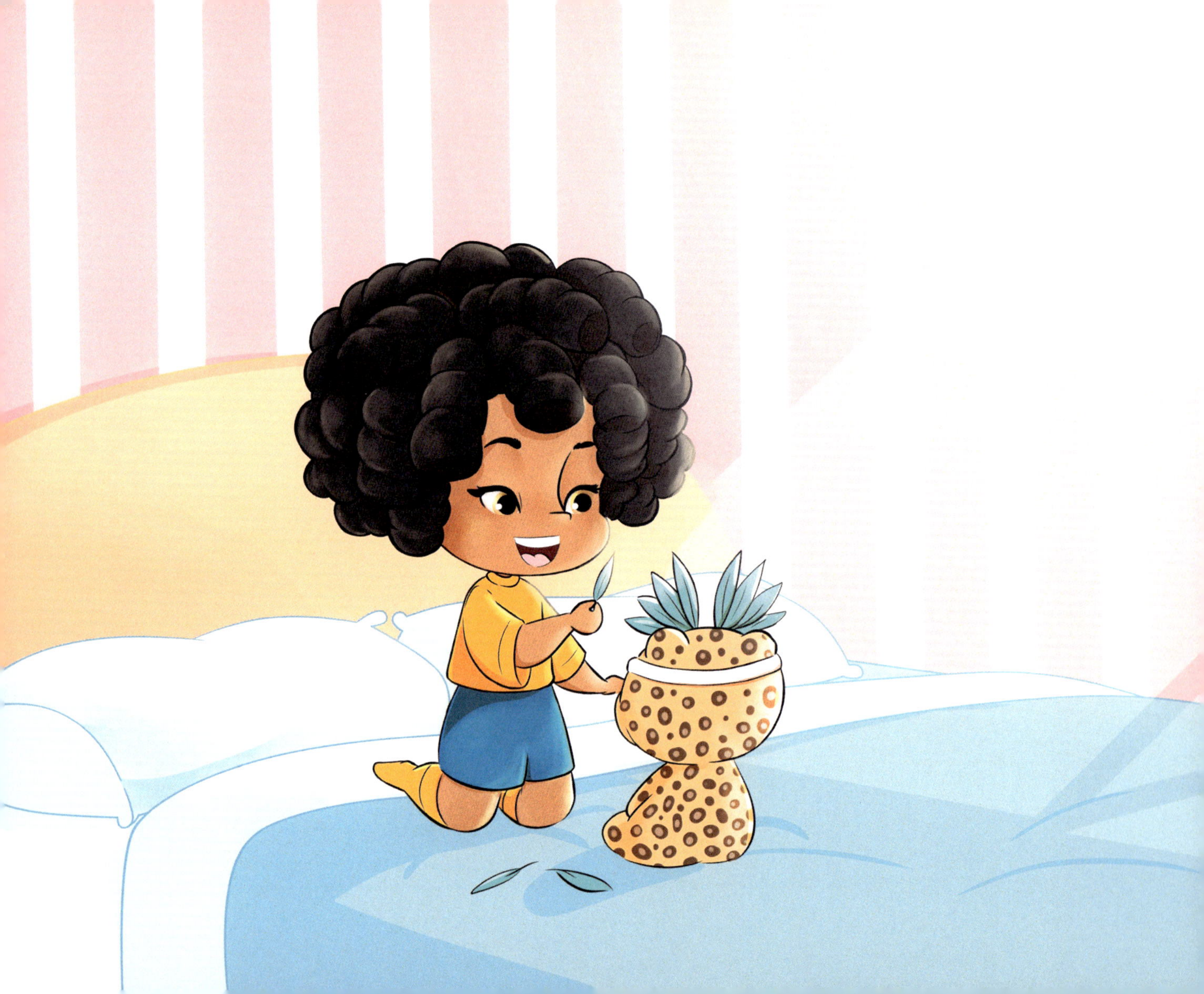

"Just one more feather and your costume is complete!" Sandy squealed with excitement as she glued the last feather onto Zooma's headband. Zooma was Sandy's favorite stuffed animal, a cheetah who traveled everywhere Sandy went. On this trip, Sandy, her mom, and Zooma were visiting Naana, who lived in Nassau, the beautiful capital city of the Bahamas. Nassau was located on the island of New Providence, one of over 700 islands in The Bahamas. Today was the annual Junior Junkanoo Carnival, so they needed to look their very best!

"Naana, I'm ready to get dressed!" called Sandy.
"I've double-stitched every part of your costume. That way, the decorations will stay in place," said Naana as she helped Sandy put on her outfit. "You know Junkanoo is one of my favorite traditions."
"It's so beautiful! I can't wait to show Mommy!" exclaimed Sandy, admiring the dark blue turquoise feathers on her dress. "Thank you!"

Sandy stood in front of the mirror, grinning ear to ear as Naana pinned her headband to her beautiful, curly bun. Her headpiece was in the shape of a three-leaf clover and decorated with turquoise jewels and feathers that matched the beautiful hues of the Caribbean Sea. Sandy was in love with her look and couldn't wait to celebrate with the new friends she hoped to make at the carnival.

"Sandy, are you ready?" asked Sandy's mom.
"Almost, Mommy, but Zooma needs his costume on, too!" replied Sandy.
Naana carefully helped Sandy get Zooma's t-shirt on, without damaging his perfect headband. Before leaving, Sandy kissed her puppy dog Chai goodbye and grabbed her backpack, which her mom had packed with swim gear and snacks.

Their hotel was only a mile away from Bay Street, where the celebration was held, but it was still a little too far and too warm to walk.
"Naana, are we going to hail a jitney?"
"No we're not, I'm driving. Hop in!"

On the way, Sandy saw Cuban amazon parrots flying above them in small groups.
"Mommy, maybe they are going to Junkanoo, too!"
When they arrived, Sandy was so excited that she grabbed Zooma by the leg and leaped out the car.

"Sandy! There will be a big crowd today. You have to hold my hand so we don't get separated," said Naana.
"I'm sorry, Naana. Can you help me strap Zooma on my backpack? He needs to be safe, too," said Sandy.
"Of course," said Naana.

Sandy triple-checked to make sure Zooma was secure and that everyone could still see his cool outfit. Then she took Naana and Mommy's hands and pulled the two women towards the island melodies.

Sandy skipped with excitement. "This is amazing! The music is so fun!"

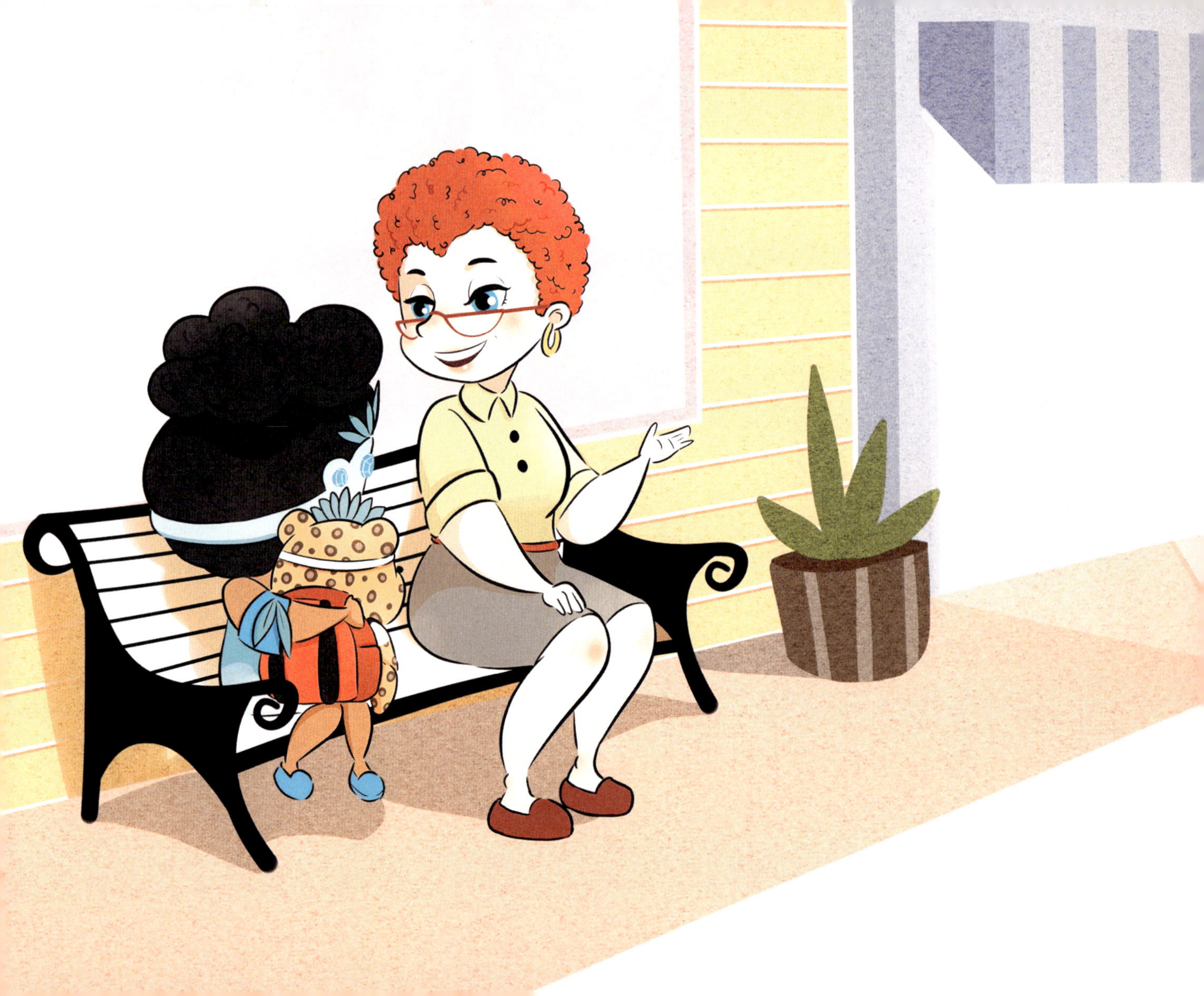

"Yes it is, little one, but do you know the meaning of Junkanoo?" asked Naana.
"No, what is it?" asked Sandy.
Realizing that this was a lesson best taught by Naana, Sandy's mom ventured off to do her favorite thing: shop! Plus, she wanted to give Sandy and Naana some time alone together.

"Sit down right here and I'll tell you," said Naana. "Junkanoo is a national festival that we Bahamians celebrate every year around Christmastime. We play different musical instruments and wear a sea of colors to show the love of our people as well as our pride as Bahamians. The festival takes place right here on Bay Street in Nassau."

"Is everyone in town invited?" Sandy was intrigued.

"Yes, and almost everyone comes. While there are several versions, the story I was told as a girl was that the name 'Junkanoo' came from an African tribal chief whom the Europeans had named John Canoe. When he and the other Africans were brought to the West Indies, Junkanoo was what they called the time of celebration during the Christmas holidays. It remains one of our grandest times of the year."

"Wow! That's so cool, Naana," said Sandy. "And children get to play and celebrate too?!"

"Children are the best part of the celebration! We hope kids like you will carry on the Junkanoo tradition and share our history with your future children. Oh, look Sandy! The Junior Junkanoo parade is starting!"

Mommy returned from shopping, and she, Sandy, and Naana watched as more than a hundred kids paraded down the street in their costumes.
Sandy yanked Zooma out of his harness and started dancing and singing. Some of the kids stopped to dance with Sandy. "Naana! This is awesome!" shouted Sandy.

After the Junior Junkanoo festival ended, Sandy, her mom, and Naana went to the beach, and were joined by a couple of the kids from the parade. They snorkeled, collected seashells, and flew a kite. Sandy even found an oyster shell with a small, pink pearl inside.

During dinner, Sandy drew pictures of all of the day's most memorable moments in her journal. In between bites of grouper and conch salad,

Sandy's mom admired her drawings. She was so entranced by her daughter's artwork that she accidently bit into a scotch bonnet pepper! "Ouch!" she yelled. Luckily, after several glasses of milk her mouth didn't burn as much.

Naana dropped Sandy and her mom off at their hotel after dinner. It was time to say goodbye.
"I'll miss you, Naana, but I'll be back soon," said Sandy.
"I'll miss you too, but I'll be there sooner! I love you!"
Sandy and her mom gave Naana one last hug before going back to their room.

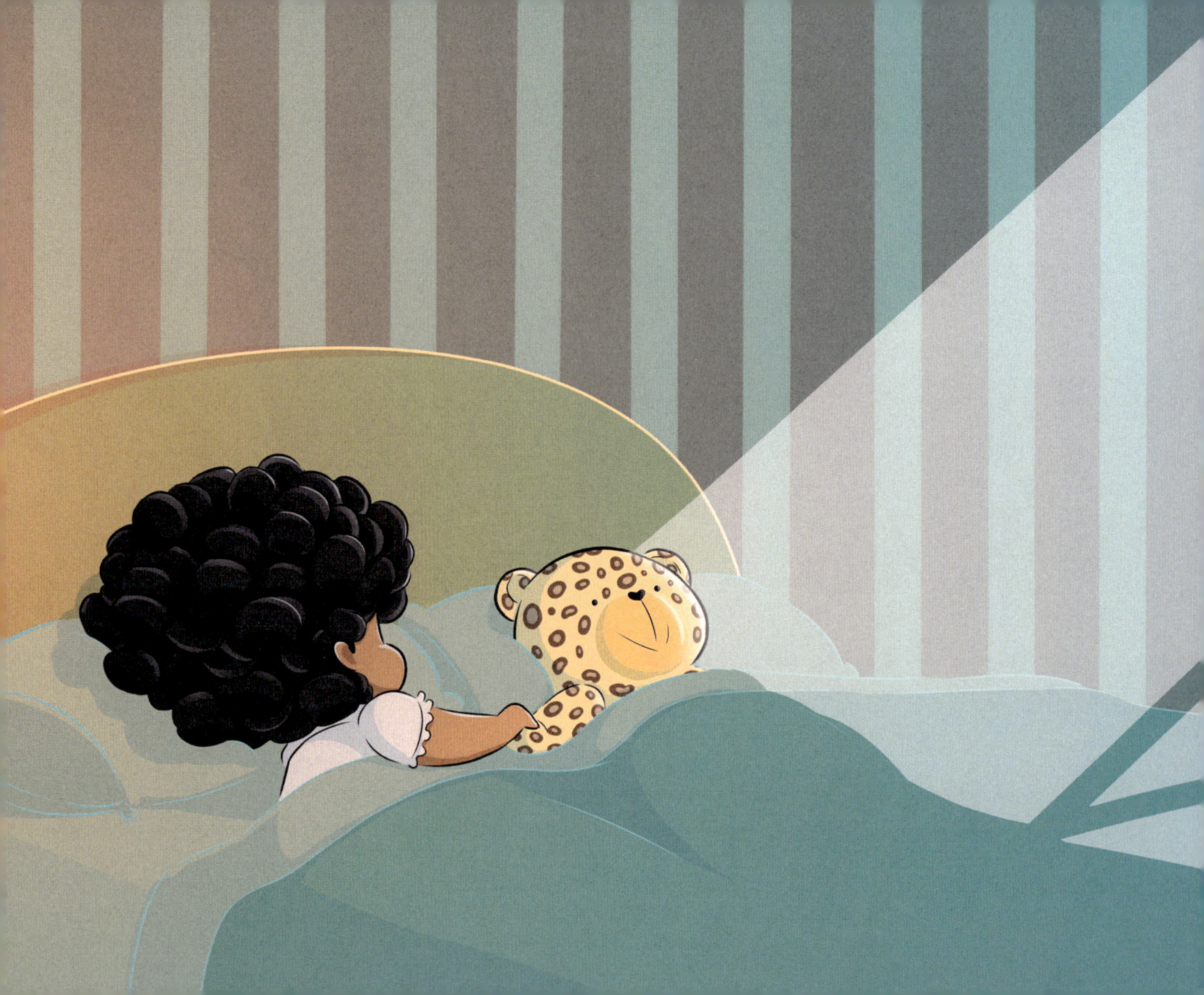

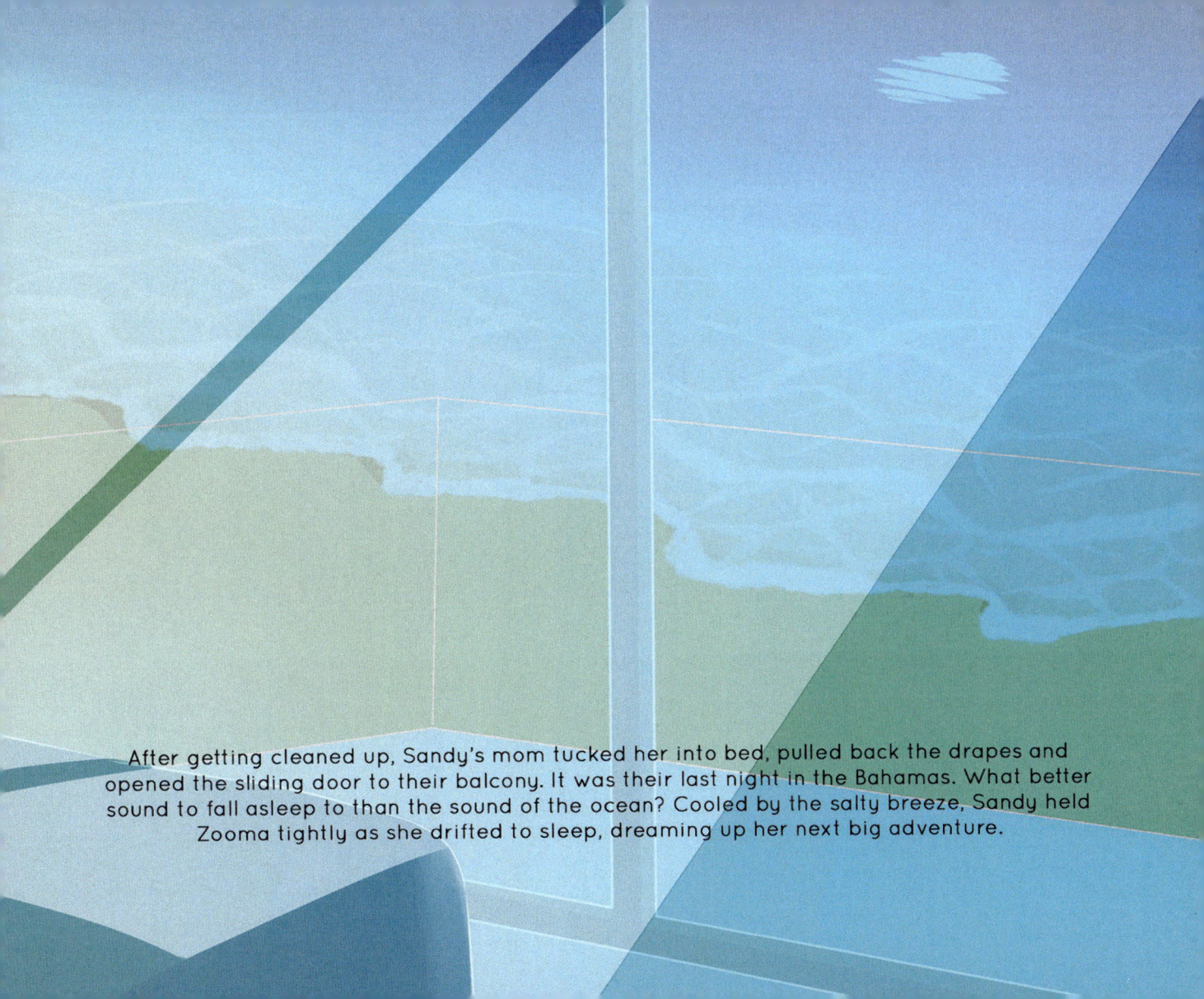

After getting cleaned up, Sandy's mom tucked her into bed, pulled back the drapes and opened the sliding door to their balcony. It was their last night in the Bahamas. What better sound to fall asleep to than the sound of the ocean? Cooled by the salty breeze, Sandy held Zooma tightly as she drifted to sleep, dreaming up her next big adventure.

GLOSSARY

Nassau - originally called Charles Towne, capital of The Bahamas, West Indies, a port on the northeastern coast of New Providence Island, and one of the world's chief pleasure resorts. The climate is temperate and the sandy beaches and scenery are beautiful. Although the city proper is comparatively small, suburbs and residential districts stretch far along the coast and into the interior.

The Bahamas - archipelago and country on the northwestern edge of the West Indies. Formerly a British colony, The Bahamas became an independent country within the Commonwealth in 1973

Junkanoo - Junkanoo parades, or "rush outs," are held annually on Boxing Day and New Year's Day in Nassau and on some of the Out Islands. Nassau's Bay Street is the site of the largest parade.

Caribbean Sea - suboceanic basin of the western Atlantic Ocean, lying between latitudes 9° and 22° N and longitudes 89° and 60° W. It is approximately 1,063,000 square miles (2,753,000 square km) in extent.

Hail - to greet or summon by calling, example: "Please hail a cab for us to take us to the store."

Cuban Amazon Parrot - The Cuban parrot is a fairly small bird only weighing about a half of a pound (Arkive). They have a height of 12 inches and a wingspan between 6.75-7.75 inches (Linné). The male birds tend to be one to four percent larger than the females (Reynolds). They are a colorful bird with a lot of color variations which is why they are often called the "rose throated parrot" (Neotropical). Read more about them here: https://sites.psu.edu/birdsofcuba/birds-of-cuba/cuban-parrot

GLOSSARY

New Providence Island - principal island of The Bahamas, West Indies. It is located between Andros Island (west) and Eleuthera Island (east). The island has a length of 21 miles (34 km) and a width of 7 miles (11 km) and is mostly flat, with swamps and several shallow lakes.

West Indies - crescent-shaped group of islands more than 2,000 miles (3,200 km) long separating the Gulf of Mexico and the Caribbean Sea, to the west and south, from the Atlantic Ocean, to the east and north. From the peninsula of Florida on the mainland of the United States, the islands stretch 1,200 miles (1,900 km) southeastward, then 500 miles (800 km) south, then west along the north coast of Venezuela on the South American mainland

Jitney - small bus that carries passengers over a regular route on a flexible schedule

Cable Beach - This beach is famous for its fabulous sand and crystal waters and for the many upscale resorts that line it.

Grouper - Groupers are widely distributed in warm seas and are often dully coloured in greens or browns, but a number are brighter, more boldly patterned fishes. Some, such as the Nassau grouper are noted for their ability to change from one to any of a number of other color patterns.

Scotch Bonnet Pepper - Most Scotch bonnets have a heat rating of 80,000-400,000 Scoville units. For comparison, most jalapeño peppers have a heat rating of 2,500 to 8,000 on the Scoville scale. However, completely sweet varieties of Scotch bonnet called cachucha peppers are grown on some of the Caribbean islands.

We have used Encyclopedia Britannica, Meriam-Webster Dictionary and the official website of The Bahamas to define these words for our readers.

MAP

Photo from Open Street Map

BAHAMIAN FRUIT SALAD
ADULT SUPERVISION NEEDED

INGREDIENTS

* Juice of 2 limes
* 2 tbsp. light corn syrup
* 2 tbsp. sherry vinegar
* 1 small pineapple
* 2 oranges
* 2 bananas, peeled
* 1/3 cup golden raisins
* 1/2 cup fresh cilantro leaves

INSTRUCTIONS

1. Whisk together lime juice, corn syrup, and sherry vinegar in a large bowl.

2. Peel, core, and remove the eyes from the pineapple, then cut into large chunks.

3. Peel oranges, carefully remove all pith, then, using a sharp paring knife, cut oranges (between membranes) into sections. Slice bananas into 1/4"-thick rounds. Add fruit to dressing, mix gently, then add raisins and ciilantro and toss well.

SAVEUR, Author Lucretia Bingham

Made in the USA
Middletown, DE
29 May 2020